ISBN 978-1-332-26404-9
PIBN 10306206

This book is a reproduction of an important historical work. Forgotten Books uses
state-of-the-art technology to digitally reconstruct the work, preserving the original format
whilst repairing imperfections present in the aged copy. In rare cases, an imperfection in
the original, such as a blemish or missing page, may be replicated in our edition. We do,
however, repair the vast majority of imperfections successfully; any imperfections that
remain are intentionally left to preserve the state of such historical works.

1 MONTH OF
FREE
READING

at
www.ForgottenBooks.com

By purchasing this book you are eligible for one month membership to ForgottenBooks.com, giving you unlimited access to our entire collection of over 700,000 titles via our web site and mobile apps.

To claim your free month visit:
www.forgottenbooks.com/free306206

orseback Riding

Horseback Riding

A Practical Guide for Beginners

Containing brief and helpful hints on how to
ride a horse, riding equipment and
the acquirement of skill and
good form in riding

By

DOROTHY LOUISE BURKETT

New York

Orange Judd Publishing Co.

London: Kegan Paul, French, Trubner & Co., Limited

1922

TO
MY FATHER

Whose sympathy and approval inspired and
encouraged its preparation, this
little volume is affectionately dedicated by
the author.

TABLE OF CONTENTS

TABLE OF CONTENTS

FOREWORD

Friends and riding pupils have frequently asked me where the fundamental principles of horseback riding might be obtained in brief form and written in simple language.

Many books, of course, have been written on the subject of equestrianism but not primarily from the viewpoint of very young riders and beginners. This fact has led to a belief that this book is needed and will be useful to all who are interested in horseback riding as a graceful, enjoyable and valuable form of exercise and recreation.

What has been written is primarily for beginners, yet it is believed that others who are lovers of horses and of the art of riding will find many things of value in the rules and exercises that are suggested.

Riding is an art based simply upon things that are learned by doing; if wrongly done, riding is ungraceful and tiresome, but done correctly, joy to the rider is as lasting as life itself.

It is my belief that the rules developed in this book are essential principles that one must follow in order to become a good rider. One may not know these principles, for the good rider acquires them unconsciously. An accomplished rider is such because he already has been doing the things that have been suggested in these pages. What follows, therefore, is nothing less or nothing more than the doing of what naturally makes horseback riding both a graceful and a delightful exercise.

From childhood I have been privileged to ride a horse. When I was a small girl, my father would put me on a horse—a safe one, of course,—and teach me the first things to do. As I grew older these riding experiences were broadened by riding in a girl's camp and in the parks of the city in which I lived.

During these formative days I was fortunate also in having instruction under a celebrated teacher of equestrianism, a Spanish gentleman of culture, whose greatest satisfaction came from helping those who appreciated his instruction and recognized the fine points in the art of riding of which he was such an enthusiastic exponent.

Still later, I was privileged to be an instructor of horseback riding at Camp Barnard, a girls' summer camp where riding is accorded an important place in the camp routine work and training. In the position of teacher I have tested out what has here been put in print. If these pages make the way a little plainer to those who earnestly want to learn how to ride a horse, my purpose will have been fully accomplished.

DOROTHY L. BURKETT.

New York, N. Y.

Nothing about riding is so important as making up your mind to control your horse. A horse knows whether its rider is afraid of him or not. This fear is conveyed to the horse by nervous use of the reins, by stiffness of seat, by the way the feet are moved in the stirrups, by speech and by other acts that actually disturb or frighten the animal.

When a rider gets on his horse he must be sure that he intends to manage his horse and not let

6

the horse manage him. If you lack this confidence, select another horse that you positively know you can control. In a surprisingly short time the rider will acquire ease and confidence and both will be conveyed to the horse. After this lesson is learned, riding will take a natural course and will be done with safety.

In riding there are two essentials that must never be forgotten: (1) to secure and keep a firm seat; and (2) to use a "light hand." Without a combination of the two no one can become a good horseman.

Almost equally important is the knowledge of the proper ac-

tion in emergencies. If a horse
runs away, do not exhaust yourself by vain pulling, but guide
him out of danger, and let him
run until he is tired.

If a horse rears, loosen the reins
and lean forward.

In case of kicking, keep his
head up as much as possible and
sit firm in the saddle.

If he stumbles, quickly draw in
the reins to help him recover.

II

APPROACHING A HORSE

A good rule never to be forgotten is always to approach a
horse from the front. Beginners
are not the only persons who
often foolishly walk up to a horse
from behind. Riders of long experience frequently commit this
fault; they become careless at
times and make the approach
from wherever they happen to
be. Some of them remember
their forgetfulness with regret.

The experienced horseman
knows that horses of tempera-

ment and mettle are easily surprised. Even an old trusty horse is apt to strike out a leg in defense, when he fancies something is happening behind him. His natural weapon is his foot and he uses it with a kick.

When you approach a horse from the front you go up to him with outstretched hand and a friendly word. There is no surprise; the horse is put at ease and you feel on safer ground with the animal. This rule applies for all occasions—when the horse is in the open, whether equipped for riding, or is running loose in paddock or box stall.

Where the horse stands in his stall, tied with halter, the approach naturally must be made in a different manner. You come to the stall and stand at the rear of the animal. By speaking a few words, calling the animal by name, all surprise is cleared away and the horse, recognizing the voice, realizes a friend, not a foe, is near him.

The horse is told to stand over as the approach is made, and if he is accustomed to it, your hand may be laid on the hip or croup, and a slight pressure given as a signal for the horse to step over to the other side of the stall. This is to make room for you to enter the stall. The horse will move to the other side if properly trained, and if not, he should be trained to do this. As you pass up toward the head of the stall, a gentle pat or two is in order.

You now loosen the halter strap or remove the halter altogether and put on the bridle. The saddle may be placed on the horse and the girths attached while the horse stands in the stall or the act of saddling may be completed elsewhere. The horse then is backed out and led to any place convenient for mounting, or he is disposed of for the moment as best serves the convenience of the person bringing him out.

III

THE START

In learning to ride much depends on making the right kind of start. If there is fear of a horse, overcome this fear. Next get astride of the horse, even though riding is not to be done at the first trial. Learn how it feels to be on a horse.

Choose for the first lessons a horse that is quiet, and for the first lessons do not be ashamed of using one that is really aged. A restive and excitable horse often lessens, instead of improves,

13

a beginner's confidence. For this reason a frantic mount should not be chosen for the first rides.

One may ride bareback for the first lesson or two; or if preferred, a saddle may be used with the stirrups crossed. This helps in two ways: it gets rid of the tendency to support the weight on the stirrups instead of the saddle, a fault that many beginners easily fall into; it trains the rider to grip with knees and thighs and so hold on, a lesson that should be learned so thoroughly that it will never be forgotten.

Avoid placing only the toe of the foot in the stirrup. Many do this, thinking it aids in rising to the trot. The fact is, the lower half of the leg shoud be held relatively stationary even in the trot. What rise there is should come from the knees up.

A better support for the feet is secured by putting the ball of the foot quite well forward in the centre of the stirrup. The English rule is to push the feet well "home," even through to the instep. This form is permissible for fast riding and when riding to the hunt, but for park riding it is not generally popular in this country.

It is not a disadvantage to use different horses, especially after a bit of progress has been made in riding. Doing this tends to strengthen one's confidence; it is, therefore, worth while not to ride the same horse time after time.

After a few lessons the novelty of riding will be over, confidence will come and each ride will improve in pleasure and enjoyment. When once one gains that confidence, he will hardly be able to wait until the next ride. A friend of mine on beginning to ride was at first afraid of a horse but one day, after I had talked to her on the subject, she summoned up enough courage to try again. Several months later I learned she was riding three times a week! She could hardly wait till her appointed hour and after a few weeks she rode every single day when the weather permitted.

"Will I fall off?" How many beginners have this as a more or less continuous fear! What if you do fall off! As one rides more and more it comes home to him that there is nothing terrible in being "thrown." Therefore forget about falling off and learn to make your horse do what you want him to do. And I might add, moreover, that there is an old saying that no one becomes a good rider until thrown at least three times.

IV

PUTTING ON THE BRIDLE

A horse accustomed to a bit and bridle that fit him will offer less opposition to having a bridle put on him than would be the case if an improper bit were in use, or the bridle were too small, thus causing discomfort or pain.

The mouth is sensitive and easily abused. The object of correct bridling is to preserve, instead of diminish the sensitiveness of the mouth, hence the right sort of bit and bridle is a

pre-requisite for efficient hand-
ling and control of the mount.

When ready to bridle the horse
you are of course standing in
proper position at the horse's
head. The bridle is lifted upwards with the left hand in front
of the face of the horse until it is
above his eyes. The right hand
is now passed over the horse's
head where the bridle is grasped
for the purpose of placing it in
position. The left hand is withdrawn and lowered to the region
of his mouth.

The mouth is opened by a
slight pressure with the thumb
and forefinger on the bars under
the lower lip, and the bit guided
into the mouth by the left hand.

Some horses readily permit the bit to be inserted while others are slow about opening the lips. If you insert the forefinger in between the lips and tickle the roof of the mouth, further resistance to admission is usually overcome.

The act of bridling is completed by lifting the bridle with the right hand up over the head, placing the poll strap back of the ears where it readily falls into place. In adjusting the throat latch remember that if drawn too tight it may cause unnecessary discomfort to the horse.

In case the animal is to be mounted at once arrange the reins backward on the neck in proper position and mount the horse. If not ready for mounting it is permissible to hold the animal, or to lead him by the reins to whatever spot is the objective point. The reins may be withdrawn from over the horse's head and used as a lead strap.

V

SADDLING THE HORSE

Whatever kind of saddle is used, make certain that the stirrups and stirrup straps are trustworthy. Many a fall has been the result of an old or imperfect stirrup strap. Get a stirrup that fits the foot. Losing a stirrup from the slipping out of the foot when taking a fast gait is annoying and may cause a mishap.

A saddle cloth under the saddle is desirable for three reasons: First, if protects the rider's garments from being soiled by perspiration of the horse; second, it absorbs perspiration under the saddle, thus aiding in keeping the pads of the saddle soft and flexible; and third, it greatly protects the horse from injury that would come with the use of the saddle next to the horse's back. Some saddles, however, are so excellently made that a saddle cloth is unnecessary.

To put on a saddle, stand at the side of the horse and place the saddle squarely over the horse's back just behind the top of the shoulders. The region on the top of the shoulders in the horse is known as the withers. You may find it less difficult if the stirrups are crossed over the top of the saddle when the saddle is put on the horse. After the girths are adjusted the stirrups are dropped into position.

Arrange the saddle cloth and saddle so that they present a neat appearance. Be sure that the blanket or pad is entirely void of any roughness or wrinkles before the saddle is put in place. Negligence in arranging the pad before placing the saddle often causes painful and troublesome sores on the horse's back.

Now reach down under the horse for the girths. A double girth is safer than a single one. First, attach the girth in front. As you tighten it the horse may "swell up" for the reason he does not want a tight corset around him.

Fasten the front girth as tight as you can. This done, reach under the horse and get the other girth and draw it up as you did with the first one. Return now to the foreward girth and take up the slack in it, drawing it tight. This done, repeat the same operations with the second or outer girth.

The last thing is the fastening of the girth. This is done after you feel certain that under no circumstances can the saddle turn when the rider is seated in it. With a little practice in adjusting the girths and making them secure no further difficulty will be experienced in making the saddle secure for any kind of riding.

It goes without saying that every real horseman knows how to saddle his horse. A groom or stable boy may do this ordinarily but there always comes a time when this knowledge and experience are greatly appreciated by the man or woman who rides a horse.

VI

THE BIT AND REINS

The double rein and bit are preferable, especially for horses of courage, or for animals that are spirited or unruly. In riding, both pairs of reins may be held in the hands, or the rider may "ride on" the snaffle, as it is called, governing the horse with the light bit. In this case the curb rein hangs slack until required, thereby saving the horse inconvenience, possibly pain, and avoiding the unnecessary hardening of the mouth.

Some riders knot the curb rein and allow it to rest on the neck of the animal, where if needed, it can readily be grasped and be brought into use.

The way the rider uses the reins is of the utmost importance. A rider whose hands convey to the horse a sympathetic touch or manner of holding the bridle reins, most easily controls the animal he is riding. A "heavy fisted" rider gets less out of a horse than another with "light hands." The heavy handed individual has most trouble with his horse, whereas light hands secure just the kind of control that brings out the best there is in the horse. A light hand is a firm hand but not rough in its use of the reins.

Much depends upon the bit. A bit suited to one horse may be entirely unsuited to another.

It is important that the bit be adjusted to the mouth of the animal, both with respect to size and width. Furthermore, the bit should be attached to the bridle in such manner as to "hang free" in the mouth and not to draw up at the sides, thus causing discomfort to the horse. When the reins hang loose, the bit should offer no pressure at any point on the horse's mouth.

VII

THE STIRRUP STRAP

The stirrup strap has much to do in the maintenance of a good seat in horseback riding. If too short, the knee is caused to bend, an effect in itself that is unsightly. A longer stirrup improves appearance in the seat and gives more ease to the mount.

Another objection against the short stirrup is the insecurity of it. It is by gripping with knees and thighs that the rider most easily keeps his seat in the saddle. This thigh gripping is lessened when the knees are forced up by short stirrups.

The jumping-jack effect so frequently observed among riders is the result of unduly short stirrups. Furthermore, this short stirrup tends to throw the body forward, causing the rider to rise up too high in the trot. Short stirrups are often responsible for lack of grace in the posture.

If the stirrups are set to the right length the rider will be sitting near to the centre of action on the horse. Short stirrups force the rider to sit to the back of the saddle which is not comfortable for horse or rider.

Four good rules for determin-

ing the proper length of stirrups
are as follows:

First.   When the leg is extended the stirrup should hang
opposite the ankle joint when the
leg is extended downwards.

Second.   When the leg is extended, raise the toes as much as
possible and adjust the stirrup
strap so that the ball of the foot
will rest in the stirrup at the
height to which the toes are
raised.

Third.   When the ball of the
foot is in the stirrup, the rider
can, keeping his ankle still bent,
so raise himself as just to clear
the saddle.

Fourth.   Before mounting put
the stirrup under the arm-pit and

adjust the stirrup strap to the same length as is the distance from the arm-pit to the finger-tips.

VIII

SPURS

Spurs are set over the heels and are fastened by a strap around the instep. They give completion to one's attire even though they are never brought into use in controlling the horse.

But spurs really are very useful. There are times when more than voice or whip is required to insure obedience of the mount. Rightly applied, the spur assists in urging a horse to go forward when unruly or frightened. Often the spur brings subjection

34

more speedily than any other method of control.

When the spur is needed, move the leg towards the horse's body, and when the spur point is within a half inch of it, gently strike it home. Use it cautiously, not roughly. When the spur strikes, have the reins well in hand.

Sharp spur points that inflict unnecessary pain are to be avoided. Keep in mind that the spur is to be a reminder of punishment to the horse if disobedient. Frequently, in the bleeding flanks, it tells a tale of the bad temper or cruel disposition of the rider.

IX

THE WHIP OR CROP

There is a rare art in carrying a whip on horseback. The manner by which it is held and used tells a story all its own.

A whip is needed not so much to punish the horse or animate him, as to control his gaits and movements. It may be pressed against the flank for controlling and guidance much in the same way as the leg is used for this purpose.

In starting, one may apply pressure with the leg and whip

thus bringing the horse up to the bit. In making a turn the pressure of the whip may be applied at the rear to keep the haunches from spreading out.

The whip should be held in the right hand and may hang at the side, or point backwards toward the hip. Avoid a heavy hand in holding the whip and do not let it take a position in which it would touch or strike the horse when not intended to do so.

X

MOUNTING

One should learn to mount from either side of his horse. Most riders prefer the left side as a general thing, but one's education is not complete until he is able to mount from the right side as well as from the left side.

Before mounting speak a few words to the horse. You have walked up to him in a quiet way and are full of anticipation and confidence yourself; let the horse be made to feel the same. A few gentle pats on the neck and face will do wonders in putting a horse at ease, especially if you speak to him gently as you do your patting.

You are now standing at his head; and to mount, you need only to move backward a step or two until you are at the shoulder, the left one. Fix the reins in the left hand and with the right hand separate a portion of the mane, winding it about the left thumb that is resting on the withers with the reins properly in place in between the fingers.

The next move is to use the right hand for aiding the left foot into the stirrup; this done, the right hand is carried upwards and placed on the saddle, the thumb and fingers grasping the pommel of the saddle. This completes the position for making the mount.

Make a springing leap, partly supporting yourself with the left leg and foot already in place in the left stirrup. As the ascent is made, the right leg is thrown well over the horse's back without bending the knee, and then drops downward on the other side, the body assumes an even posture, the right hand is released of its hold, the right foot is placed in its stirrup, and the reins are quickly grasped by both hands or adjusted in the left—and the act of mounting reaches its completion.

MOUNTING

All this is done in a surprisingly short time, but while doing it make sure not to produce any reaction on the bit. During the period the rein is held tight enough to keep the horse standing quietly.

XI

THE HANDS

It is by the hand or hands on the rein that a horse is more or less directed, and certainly by the hands he is kept in control. Skilled riders for the most part hold the reins in the left hand. Beginners should use both hands, holding the reins on either side with the hand on that side.

Many experienced riders like to ride in this manner and it is perfectly correct for them so to do. It depends somewhat on the individual and somewhat on the horse. When a perfectly docile animal is ridden and which is completely submissive to the rider's mastery, the left hand will quite well suffice. But where great care is necessary, either because of the horse or of the roads, holding the reins in the two hands is safest.

Youthful riders, because of their small hands, should always take the reins in the two hands; and women riders usually find this manner of holding the reins the most satisfactory. Experienced riders follow both methods, changing from one to the other as the mood comes on them.

The hands are employed to keep the horse in subjection, and

in turning. In turning, if the horse is not well trained, the rein on the side to which the horse is to go will be gently pulled, thus indicating the direction. A horse well educated in riding methods may be turned by pressing the rein on either side of the neck. He is then said to be "bridle wise."

The reins are held in the left hand thus: thumb up and pointing to the horse's ears; reins between the fingers, one rein for each if four reins are used; the little finger directly above the pommel of the saddle, near to it but not more than a few inches above it.

The hands are held a few

inches to the front of the rider, giving plenty of room for pulling in the reins without changing the grasp on them. All reins should be clasped between the thumb and first finger. Learn to press the thumb on the reins as it is the controller ; back of it lies all the power and strength in holding the reins. If the thumb does not grasp the reins firmly, the rider is likely to lose his reins and then he comes up against danger.

This manner of holding the reins enables the rider to carry the elbow close to his side, which is the graceful way to carry it. Very frequently one observes riders with the back of the hand turned up, the knuckles upwards;

instead of greater ease, and more power coming to the hands, the reverse is true. Spreading elbows are, therefore, to be avoided.

As one rides more and more he uses his hands with greater ease and therefore with more freedom. The hands acquire a dexterity, or "lightness," which accomplishment is really a firmness of the hands that enables the skillful rider to direct his mount with such sensitive touch as to give absolute control of every movement.

HORSEBACK RIDING

XII

THE LEGS

If the stirrup straps are of proper length and the rider clearly understands what it means to depend upon the thighs and knees for safety in the seat, the legs will assume their proper position and greatly help in keeping the seat and maintaining a proper posture of the body.

But the legs serve other purposes also. They help to guide and assist the horse in his movements no less so than the hands. The hands control the movements of the forequarters, the legs of the hind quarters. Indeed, the only control of the horse's hind parts rests in the use of the rider's legs.

When the rider's legs are pressed against the horse's sides, the horse is induced to move forward or move his hind feet forward. Thus, without words, the horse is given a signal as to what is wanted.

By placing one leg backwards, say just behind the saddle girths, and putting gentle pressure on the leg, the rider will turn the horse from the rear around the front legs from that side. Like results are obtained for the other side when the leg on that side is similarly placed for the opposite effect.

The legs serve also in turning. In doing this equal pressure is given—one leg forward of the girths and the other to the rear. The hand on the rein should aid the legs in bringing about the desired result.

In still another way the legs may be brought into use. The rider shifts his weight to one side by partially standing in one stirrup, releasing all weight on the other leg. This action will cause the horse to raise his legs and feet on the side from which the weight was lifted.

As both horse and rider are educated to understand the ser-

vice and importance of these
simple hints, the pleasure of riding increases proportionally.

XIII

THE FEET

The assistance that the feet render in riding comes so naturally in connection with the treatment of other topics that there is left little to say here except as to the proper form by which the feet are to be carried in the stirrups.

There are three rules that one should never forget: First, the feet must always be carried nearly parallel to the horse's body, with the toe turned out very little, and the heel pressed downward.

51

Secondly, the ball of the foot must rest firmly on the stirrup. The exception to this rule is in strenuous riding, such as riding to the hunt, racing, polo, and jump- ing, in which cases the foot is allowed to "go home."

Third, the feet must not be flapped in and out, or backwards and forwards.

Nothing is so indicative of bad form as any departure from these three rules; also, nothing is so ex- pressive of correct riding educa- tion and discipline as a constant observance of them.

XIV

TURNING

The hand and leg are both employed in turning. The hand by means of the pull on one rein centers attention on the direction while the pressure of the leg influences a uniform movement from the hind quarters.

In turning the horse in any pace, the rider should recollect that he is not simply to pull the horse around by the head. The legs should be held sufficiently close to the sides of the horse and when the rider desires to turn, the leg on the side from which it is desired to turn, should be carried back of the girths and be pressed against the horse at the same time that the hand pulls the rein on the side to which the direction is to be taken. This will enable the horse to turn gracefully and to retain his lightness.

Guided by the legs and hands simultaneously in turning, the horse is assured of an equilibrium which will insure safety to both horse and rider.

Often a beginner turns his horse too quickly and in so doing causes the horse to step on his own feet. This gives rise to what is known as "corked feet." A wound of this kind, which often

TURNING

is serious, may be entirely avoided in making a turn by bringing the horse around in a slow, easy and graceful movement.

XV

BACKING

Many times come when it is desirable "to back" one's mount. Too frequently backing is done awkwardly and ungracefully when the reverse ought to be the case. A rider's cleverness and degree of horsemanship is indicated by the ease and mastery by which a horse is backed out of difficulty or into a better position for a few minutes of waiting.

In backing, make certain that the horse is not twisted or standing in a curve. Make him stand straight, the croup in line with the rider's shoulders, the horse light in hand, and easy in the bit. Now press gently against the two sides in such a way as to cause the horse to lift one of his hind legs, the light bit being held sufficiently strong to prevent his advancing.

At once when a hind leg is raised, pull in on the curb rein which will cause the horse to replace the raised leg on the ground but at the rear of the place where the foot originally had been. These movements are to be continued until the desired position is reached. If the horse turns to right or left bring him into place by the proper pressure of the leg and by aid of the light bit.

To walk backwards is good practice for both rider and horse and after a brief experience it may be done easily and gracefully. It is a good test in the education of both horse and rider.

XVI

THE HALT

Only by practice can one fully understand the rare acquirement of bringing his horse to a halt from a rapid pace. One of the prettiest accomplishments is to make a quick halt from a fast pace as, for example, the gallop. All skillful riders effect this without difficulty, for they and their horses are reasonably well trained.

The secret of making the halt from a rapid pace is to give the command when the hind legs are under the horse. For the walk or slow trot this rule is not important, but in rapid paces it is.

The aim in halting is to distribute the shock to fore and hind legs. A sudden halt made when the horse is on the front legs may lead to a fall. Stopping on the front legs gives horse and rider an unnecessary jolt which is disagreeable and dangerous for both.

A good rule is to have the hind legs under the body when the horse stops so that they receive a part of the shock, and the full shock is not forced upon the front legs. The horse is touched gently with the spurs when the hind legs are forward, and immediately the reins are drawn in. This method gives a graceful halt and inconveniences neither horse nor rider.

Inexperienced riders often draw the reins with a sudden pull without communicating the purpose in any manner to the horse. Unfamiliarity with the right way of halting has precipitated many a rider over the horse's head.

A safe rule for beginners is to bring the horse gradually to a walk from whatever pace the horse is making and then by word or drawing-in of the reins the rider conveys the signal to come to a halt.

XVII

THE WALK

The walk is the gait that should first be attempted on starting a ride, either by beginner or experienced horseman. This insures the rider's confidence in the horse and allows him time to study the animal's disposition. If, of course, the rider is well acquainted with his mount, this is not necessary, but in general when one rides a horse entirely strange to him he should make that horse walk for a few minutes, turning him in different directions, and causing him to stop and then go at will.

When he has his mount under control to his satisfaction he is then ready to try other slow gaits, or the trot and canter. These latter gaits will be more enjoyable if the rider feels at ease on his mount. The beginner, however, should let the walk be the only gait for the first lesssons at least.

The walk is the simplest of all gaits. It is only necessary to say of it that when resorted to as a resting or breathing time for a weary horse, it should be performed with animation, the head being kept in position and the action made lively and firm.

But after fast traveling on the

road it is at times desirable to allow the horse's head to drop and the whole muscular system of the horse's body to become relaxed. He must be ready instantly, however, to regain his firmness in case of a fallen step.

The rider can help the horse even in walking. It is advisable always to have a fairly firm grasp upon the reins and if the horse should happen to stumble, the rider can assist in the recovery by quickly drawing them in.

In changing gaits, usually the start is made from the walk, although a horse ought to respond to any gait to which the rider desires to change.

In going from a walk to a trot,

the rider should slacken the reins, and rise in the saddle; and for the canter he should give the horse free rein and lean well forward in the saddle.

A well-trained horse will change from one gait to another directly without going back to the walk. If, for instance, the rider is trotting and wishes to canter, he should lean forward in the saddle and give the horse full rein. In other words, to change the gait, the rider simply assumes the position that he would have in the new gait and the horse falls naturally into that new gait.

XVIII

THE TROT

Unquestionably, the trot is the fashionable gait in horseback riding. It is less easy for the rider and for the horse than a well gathered canter and it is for both an artificial gait. Both horse and rider need practice before the gait can be performed gracefully. It is in the trot that posture so frequently takes on an unsightly appearance; the rider should sit up straight, head held high, chin in, as if the world belongs to him.

When the horse's right foreleg goes forward, rise up, pressing the stirrup with the ball of the foot and then come down on the saddle when the left foreleg goes forward. By practice this posting will become very natural and the rider will wonder why he never did it before. Once you get it the trick will never leave you. Always go with the horse; go up with him; then down; up-down, up-down.

Counting, it runs:

1 - 2, 1 - 2, 1 - 2.

Right foreleg forward, - 1; left foreleg, - 2.

Repeat this to yourself and you will find it helps greatly.

It is in the trot that you see so many riders riding as if they were jumping jacks, bounding up in the seat and coming down again on the saddle. In rising one should barely leave the saddle. The thickness of the hand between the saddle and the body is an old rule of experienced horsemen. To insure this, the length of the stirrup strap should be correct as to length. I myself like a long stirrup as I find I have then better thigh support.

Properly adjusted, the stirrup straps make easy posting possible. There follows perfect rhythm between horse and rider, otherwise, lacking this harmonious motion, the rider is jolted up and down, bumping and pitching, as each step is taken.

THE TROT

I repeat again: make certain that the stirrup straps are of proper length—and go with the horse. Do not work too hard, for body tenseness greatly diminishes the pleasure that comes from riding.

XIX

GALLOP AND CANTER

The gallop and canter are entirely different paces. The gallop is a succession of short leaps, whereas the canter is a movement of the front and hind legs successively, yet the transition of one to the other is so gradual that it would be difficult exactly **to** fix it.

The riding horse is bred to raise his feet well up in the air. This is particularly essential with the canter, which is a slow high bound. In taking this pace the horse is made to gallop and then to go slow.

Like the trot, the gallop or can-ter is a popular gait. It is easy on the horse, and besides it gives the rider much more exercise than does the rack. The style of riding in both gaits is very much the same.

In both the gallop and canter the knees and thighs should in all cases grasp the horse, but not with so much power as to render the horse uncomfortable.

In these gaits the motion of the horse is very much increased over the walk or trot and hence proportionally greater is the necessity for caution to secure a safe, firm seat.

HORSEBACK RIDING

A beginner should not attempt the canter or gallop until he feels safe with the trot, and has gained perfect confidence in his ability to keep his seat.

It is usually best not to gallop, or even to use the slower pace of canter, in a city park. Accidents constantly occur, the horse becoming frightened at the sight of many people and vehicles; if the rider is inexperiencd, the horse is likely to take the bit in his mouth and run.

If one desires to gallop and canter, he should go on a long, open road, preferably a dirt road, and one where there is but little traffic. On such roads, with a little experience, the rider will enjoy the fast gaits to the utmost. It is wonderful exercise.

The inexperienced rider should always canter or gallop up a hill and walk down.

In cantering up, the rider helps the horse up; in walking down, the rider may assist in keeping the horse from stumbling.

XX

OTHER RIDING GAITS

There remain two other gaits that frequently are seen on the road or in the parks. These are the step-and-pace and the rack or single foot.

In the step-and-pace, the motion is first a little faster than in the walk. In it the forelegs of the horse have the motion of the slow canter and the hind legs the motion of the trot. Since this is not a natural gait it is a difficult one to teach a horse to keep.

The single foot, often called the

rack, is the result of the horse planting his feet in the same way as in the step-and-pace. It is the same kind of gait, only faster.

In these two gaits the rider sits well down in the saddle. They are restful gaits for the rider but rather tiresome for the horse.

To go from a walk to either of these paces, the rider sits well down in the saddle, keeps the reins taut and urges the horse out of the walk.

XXI

DISMOUNTING

One may leave the saddle by reversing the movements for mounting. Briefly, this is done as follows:

Holding the reins and crop in the left hand, the right is placed on the pommel of the saddle; the right foot is now withdrawn from the stirrup; the right leg, held reasonably straight, is thrown backwards and carried over the horse's croup, with care exercised so as not to strike the horse. The circuit of the right leg is continued and when it has been carried over the region of the croup it is lowered to the ground.

As these movements are progressing, the rider is in the act of lowering, or already has partly lowered himself from his seat in the saddle, so that by the time the foot touches the ground his own body has followed, avoiding any great stretch of the leg or any unsightly appearance of his person in the descent.

The act of dismounting is completed by withdrawing the left foot from its stirrup through the aid of the right hand. The left stirrup should not be permitted to flap against the horse's flank.

This is common, but it is not good form.

Many agile riders pride themselves on dismounting in another manner, thus: Both feet are taken from the stirrups and both hands placed at the front of the saddle. By means of a spring from the wrists, the saddle and horse are cleared, the rider landing on his feet near the horse. One may dismount on either side as he chooses, but in any case keep hold on the reins with the hand that is resting on the withers.

Another simple method of dismounting is to bring the right leg over the front of the saddle to the left side and then jump down.

DISMOUNTING

Boys usually find this method very speedy, and they are apt to use it at all times. It is permissible for anyone to dismount in this way as it shows the agility of the rider.

XXII

BAD MANNERS

It is bad manners to cluck at a horse, to shake the reins with the hands, or to flap the stirrups in and out or back and forth, with the feet in them.

Many terms are used by different riders in starting and stopping the horse. The terms one should use naturally depend upon those to which the horse is most accustomed.

To cluck at a horse involves many dangers. If several people are riding together and a person in the rear should cluck to his horse, the horses in the lead would hear the clucking and immediately start up in a more rapid gait. A person in the lead may be fixing a stirrup, or not paying particular attention to his horse, and when his mount suddenly begins to trot, canter or run, if he is not a skilled rider, he may be thrown.

Always think of the other person and how he might be harmed by your unthinking cluck to your horse.

Of course the ideal way is to signal by pressure on reins or with the legs, but this is generally impossible where the same horse is used by many riders and no two riders use the same manner of communication.

The same is true with respect to gaits. A horse under ordinary circumstances starts out in a walk. If the horse does not know the signal or the word for taking another gait, naturally he cannot respond to what the rider wants done. Touching up with the whip will increase the pace, but what pace the horse will take is dependent upon the mood or previous teaching of the horse.

Do not shake the reins in order to start up your horse but use the crop, or touch up with the spurs. That is what these are made for, and the sooner one learns to use them the better.

BAD MANNERS

To flap the stirrups is undoubt-edly one of the most unpardon-able faults. Keep the leg stiff from knee downward and avoid letting it sway to and fro.

XXIII

THE SEAT

Every horseback rider is interested in two things: how to ride with safety and how to ride well. The hints and exercises heretofore suggested have been presented to accomplish both of these results. A few additional words remain yet to be said about the seat, for the reason that in it are centered not only security on the horse but also the appearance of the rider. The rider's posture on his horse when in action tell the story.

84

THE SEAT

It is in the seat, in the rider's poise, in his posture when sitting in the saddle on the horse, in the carriage of his body and in his manner of riding that personality and charm are reflected and the skill and the mastery of the mount most clearly portrayed.

Don Quixote understood the meaning of this kind of good riding. In one of his lectures to Sancho he said "the seat on a horse's back makes some people look like gentlemen and others like grooms." These words convey an unquestioned meaning as to what one ought to do and how to do it when riding a horse.

When a rider becomes thoroughly at home on a horse he will

to a large degree ride independently of his hold on the reins. This will come about from right use of his whole body, not of the hands and legs only, but also of the trunk above the waist. Every rider should so school himself in training the upper portion of his body that he can lean far to the right or the left, lie forward on the horse's neck or backwards on his croup, restoring his position without pulling on the reins or interfering with his seat in the saddle.

Equally important when riding is keeping the spine straight. "Don't slouch" is so obvious as hardly to be necessary to say. Were it not a fact that many riders do slouch, this fault would not be mentioned. The right way is to sit straight, with the head up and the chin in, and maintain the body with a suppleness that suggests grace, ease and experience. The rider will then feel at home on his horse bcause he is at home on him.

At home on the horse! To ride well! To tell how these two ends and all they mean may be attained is the purpose of this little book. It will best fulfill its mission by emphasizing at all times gentle bearing, a graceful appearance and a genial personality in riding. This noble exercise is truly a fine art and is

worthy of all the patience and
perseverance expended in mas-
tering it.

CPSIA information can be obtained
at www.ICGtesting.com
Printed in the USA
BVOW06s1040180917

495170BV00019B/486/P